THE USBORNE YOUNG SCIENTIST
EVOLUTION

Barbara Cork and Lynn Bresler

Designed by Sue Mims

Consultants Mark Ridley
Anne Hollifield and Gail Vines

Contents

Illustrated by
Chris Lyon, Martin Newton, Bernard Robinson, Chris Shields, Sue Stitt
Christina McInerney, Patti Pearce, Ian Jackson, Jan Nesbitt,
David Webb, Peter Bull, Alan Harris, Phil Weare, Brenda Haw

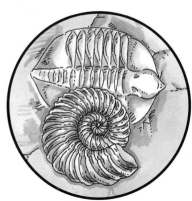

The question of life on Earth

How and when did life begin on our planet? Why is there such an incredible variety of plants and animals living on the Earth today? How did living things come to be suited to their particular way of life? Many people believe that the answer to these questions is that life on Earth developed by a process called evolution. Most scientists believe this is the best explanation for the variety of life today, using the evidence from fossils (the preserved remains of plants and animals) and from studying how plants and animals live today.

The variety of life on Earth

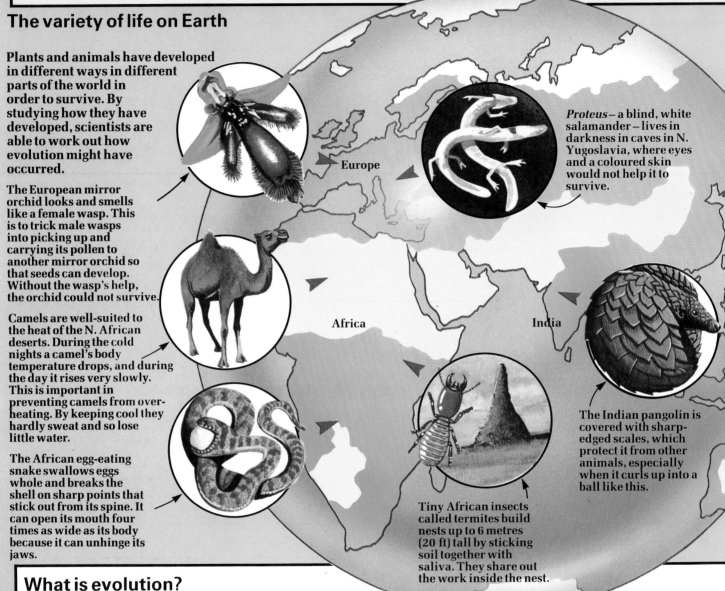

Plants and animals have developed in different ways in different parts of the world in order to survive. By studying how they have developed, scientists are able to work out how evolution might have occurred.

The European mirror orchid looks and smells like a female wasp. This is to trick male wasps into picking up and carrying its pollen to another mirror orchid so that seeds can develop. Without the wasp's help, the orchid could not survive.

Camels are well-suited to the heat of the N. African deserts. During the cold nights a camel's body temperature drops, and during the day it rises very slowly. This is important in preventing camels from over-heating. By keeping cool they hardly sweat and so lose little water.

The African egg-eating snake swallows eggs whole and breaks the shell on sharp points that stick out from its spine. It can open its mouth four times as wide as its body because it can unhinge its jaws.

Europe

Proteus – a blind, white salamander – lives in darkness in caves in N. Yugoslavia, where eyes and a coloured skin would not help it to survive.

Africa

India

The Indian pangolin is covered with sharp-edged scales, which protect it from other animals, especially when it curls up into a ball like this.

Tiny African insects called termites build nests up to 6 metres (20 ft) tall by sticking soil together with saliva. They share out the work inside the nest.

What is evolution?

The theory of evolution explains how plants and animals have gradually changed into new, different kinds of plants and animals over long periods of time. Many different processes are involved in evolution, and this book is designed to show how they all fit together.

 DNA

The most important of the processes are:
The chemical code of instructions (called DNA), which is inside every living thing. If mistakes are made to the code, new life forms might evolve. You can read about DNA and how it works on pages 10-13.

The environment (surroundings) in which plants and animals live can affect their chances of survival, which can also lead to change. This is called natural selection, which you can read about on pages 6-7.

   Fossil remains

Looking at rocks and fossils (see pages 20-21) has also helped towards understanding how evolution works, because they provide a record of extinct forms of life, as shown on pages 22-25.

Religious beliefs

All religious beliefs are a matter of faith and cannot be tested scientifically. In some religions (such as the Jewish faith, Christianity, Islam and parts of the Hindu faith), it is believed that a God created all living things and directs their development.

Other religious beliefs (such as Jainism, Buddhism and some Chinese religions) involve a world that is without beginning or end. You can learn more about these different beliefs on the next page.

The Biblical creation story in Genesis is interpreted in different ways, some of which you can read about on page 17. On the same page, you can also see some of the ideas early peoples had about how the Earth was created and developed.

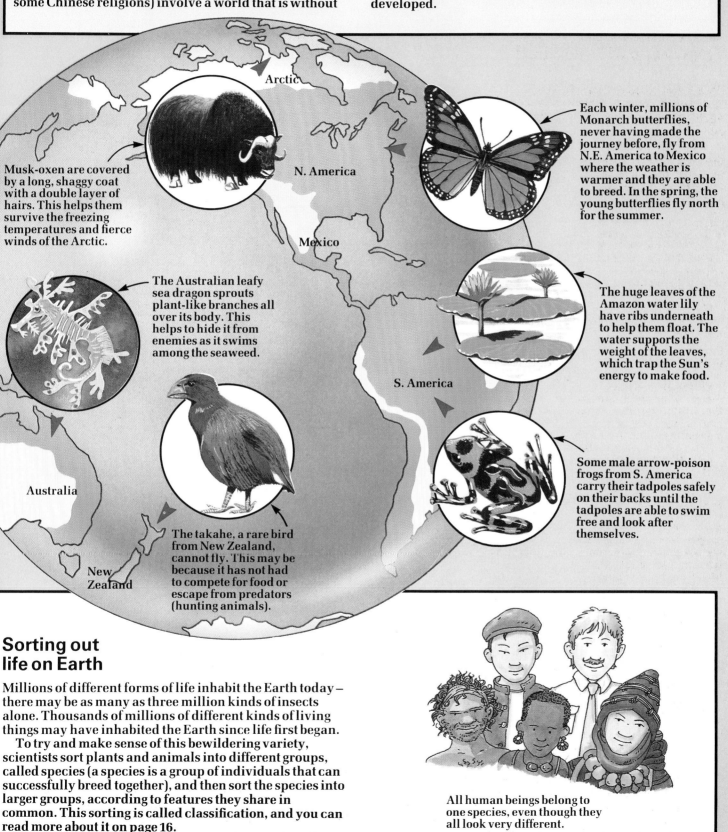

Arctic

N. America

Mexico

Musk-oxen are covered by a long, shaggy coat with a double layer of hairs. This helps them survive the freezing temperatures and fierce winds of the Arctic.

Each winter, millions of Monarch butterflies, never having made the journey before, fly from N.E. America to Mexico where the weather is warmer and they are able to breed. In the spring, the young butterflies fly north for the summer.

The Australian leafy sea dragon sprouts plant-like branches all over its body. This helps to hide it from enemies as it swims among the seaweed.

The huge leaves of the Amazon water lily have ribs underneath to help them float. The water supports the weight of the leaves, which trap the Sun's energy to make food.

S. America

Australia

New Zealand

The takahe, a rare bird from New Zealand, cannot fly. This may be because it has not had to compete for food or escape from predators (hunting animals).

Some male arrow-poison frogs from S. America carry their tadpoles safely on their backs until the tadpoles are able to swim free and look after themselves.

Sorting out life on Earth

Millions of different forms of life inhabit the Earth today – there may be as many as three million kinds of insects alone. Thousands of millions of different kinds of living things may have inhabited the Earth since life first began.

To try and make sense of this bewildering variety, scientists sort plants and animals into different groups, called species (a species is a group of individuals that can successfully breed together), and then sort the species into larger groups, according to features they share in common. This sorting is called classification, and you can read more about it on page 16.

All human beings belong to one species, even though they all look very different.

3

Thinking about evolution...

Across these two pages, you can trace the history of the most important ideas about the origin and diversity of life on Earth. You can see how religious and philosophical ideas of a perfect and unchanging world began to be challenged by scientists from the 16th century onwards. This led to Darwin's theory in the 19th century and to 20th century discoveries in genetics.

Creation myths and religion

The creation myths, dating from about 3000BC, are the earliest written ideas about the origin of the world. A popular idea of the Ancient Egyptians was that the sun god, Re, created the world from a dark, watery chaos. A myth from Mesopotamia tells of a god creating the universe from the body of a dead monster.

There are two accounts of the creation of the world in the Book of Genesis in the Bible, both written more than 500 years BC. The first describes how God created the world in six days; the second concerns the creation of human beings from the first man and woman – Adam and Eve.

18th century

In the 18th century, many people thought that God directed the natural processes that shaped the Earth. Scientific discoveries suggested the Earth was much older than Biblical estimates. Explorers found a huge variety of species not mentioned in the Bible and the discovery of fossils that were unlike any modern forms suggested that God had allowed some of his creatures to become extinct (die out).

Buffon worked out the age of the Earth as at least 168,000 or even half a million years old. He did not believe in evolution, but brought the idea into science by discussing problems such as extinction and how species form.

Linnaeus developed a system of classifying living things, which he thought revealed the order of God's design.

A 17th century scientist

19th century

At the beginning of the 19th century, Lamarck put forward the first theory of evolution, which most people did not accept. They believed in the unchanging, recently created world of the Bible or in a world of natural laws created and controlled by God. In 1859, Darwin published his theory of natural selection, which became the basis for the modern theory of evolution.

This plaice is suited to its environment, the seabed.

Paley suggested that living things were so well suited to their environment, they must have been designed by an intelligent creator.

Cuvier believed in an original creation which was wiped out from time to time by catastrophes in different parts of the world. After each catastrophe, plants and animals from nearby areas filled the gaps.

Lamarck believed living things had evolved gradually from the simplest to the most complex. He suggested that in each generation living things could change their characteristics to cope with the environment, and pass these changes on to their offspring.

In the 1820s and 30s, geologists argued about whether God controlled natural processes. Some thought the fossil evidence showed gradual change through time, others believed in separate creations throughout time, with species becoming extinct and being replaced by new ones.

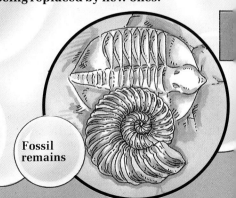

Fossil remains

Jainism and Buddhism began about 600BC, and teach that the world has no beginning or end and is ruled by vital energy forces.

Islam began in Mecca about AD600 and its followers believe one God made heaven and earth and human beings.

Hinduism developed about 5,000 years ago. Most Hindus believe the world was created by one or more gods.

Ancient Greeks

The early Greek philosophers were the first to suggest that the world was created and controlled by natural processes and chance rather than by a God. They also believed in a perfect world which stayed the same through all time. So they were interested in the beginning of things but not change or evolution afterwards.

Plato (left) and Aristotle (right)

Their ideas, especially those of Plato and Aristotle, lasted for nearly 2,000 years.

According to Plato, the only things that really existed were "forms", which were fixed forever.

Plato's pupil, Aristotle, was the first to observe a system in nature. He arranged living things according to their degree of "perfection" in a Ladder of Nature. God was at the top and humans were half way down.

17th century

In the 17th century, telescopes revealed that Space seemed to have no limits and early microscopes showed tiny creatures with amazing and complex structures. There was a widespread belief that microscopic creatures could be created from non-living matter. But scientists still tried to make their discoveries fit with the Bible.

16th century

In the 16th century, people began to question religious beliefs. They rediscovered the works of the Greeks, explorers found strange new animals and plants and the first scientific discoveries were made.

A new plant discovery

Middle Ages

In Europe during this period, people believed the world had been created recently by God. Plants and animals had been put into the world to serve people. There was more interest in the purpose and will of God than the study of nature. But Islamic philosophers, such as Averroes, suggested a world in which creation continually took place.

Charles Darwin

Charles Darwin also believed in evolution from simple to more complex creatures, but by natural selection (that is, those individuals best adapted to their environment survive to pass on their characteristics), rather than by the actions of God. Alfred Russel Wallace came up with the same idea.

20th century

Early in the 20th century, discoveries in genetics (how characteristics are controlled and passed on) at first seemed to discredit Darwins's ideas. However, by the 1920s a new "synthetic" theory had been worked out, which brought together genetics, mathematical predictions and an updated version of Darwin's natural selection theory. In the 1950s the structure of the chemical in the genes (DNA) was discovered and by the 1960s the code of instruction carried by DNA was worked out (see pages 10-11). These discoveries led scientists in the 1970s and 80s to think of natural selection as working at the gene level, the most successful genes being those that had the most copies of themselves in the population.

Some people do not believe in evolution. Creationists believe God created every species, each of which has not evolved or died out.

Researchers are still trying to answer questions such as: How did life begin? Does life evolve by gradual or sudden changes, or both? How important is chance in evolution? How do genes control the way living things develop, function and behave?

5

Darwin's theory of natural selection

Charles Darwin put forward his theory of natural selection to explain how evolution could have happened. He realized that plants and animals must be able to pass on their characteristics to their offspring, although he knew nothing about how inheritance[1] works. He thought that the variety between individual members of a species[2] would mean that some members would be better adapted than others to their particular environment, and would be more likely to survive and pass on their helpful characteristics.

However, natural selection does not automatically lead to change. A well-adapted population may stay the same because the most typical individuals are more likely to survive and pass on their characteristics. Natural selection may also keep variety in a population, as a characteristic that is harmful in one situation may be useful in another. Some situations are so complex that other factors, which are not yet understood, may be involved.

Darwin's ideas

1. *Most species produce far more offspring than could possibly survive.* One pair of mice could produce about 40 babies a year and these babies could have offspring of their own after only six weeks. Imagine what would happen if all those mice survived and kept breeding . . .

2. *An individual's chances of survival will be affected by the environment in which it lives.* The environment includes the weather, finding food and a mate, finding somewhere to live, and other animals and plants.

Which mice are more likely to be caught by the owl?

3. *Individuals vary. Some will be better adapted than others to their environment and will stand a better chance of surviving.* Darwin did not know what caused variation – we now know it is caused by mutations and the mixing up of genes during sexual reproduction (see pages 10-13).

The dark-coloured mice stand more chance of surviving to pass on their genes.

4. *If the better-adapted individuals survive long enough to reproduce . . . and if they pass the characteristics that helped them to survive on to their offspring . . . their offspring will also stand a better chance of surviving.* This idea is sometimes called the "survival of the fittest".

Eventually there are more dark-coloured mice than light-coloured mice.

Evidence of natural selection

. . . in S. America . . . in Africa

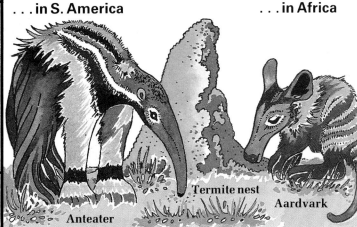

Termite nest Aardvark Anteater

Both these animals feed on ants and termites. They have strong front legs and claws to dig into the nest, and long noses and sticky tongues to find the insects and lick them up.

Darwin knew that plants and animals that live in similar surroundings look similar and cope with surviving in a similar way (as shown above). He saw this as evidence of adaptation to the environment by natural selection.

An amazing example is the 110 breeds of dog that people have developed from the wolf over 14,000 years. All dogs are still one species though, and can usually breed together.

Darwin found further evidence to support his theory from looking at domesticated plants and animals. People have deliberately changed these by breeding together specially chosen individuals. This is called artificial selection, and shows how the characteristics of plants and animals can be changed over many generations.

1. See page 12 for how inheritance works.
2. See pages 14-16 to find out more about species.

Changing with the times

If the surroundings change, the characteristics of a population may also change as a result of natural selection. This is called directional selection, and the most obvious cases nowadays are caused by the actions of humans. One example is the case of the peppered moths.

In 19th-century Britain, the tree trunks on which peppered moths rested during the day became blackened when pollution from the factories killed off the light-coloured lichens covering the trees. But the colour of the moths' wings changed over the generations to match their new surroundings, as you can see here. Since pollution was reduced in the mid-1950s, the proportion of silvery moths has gradually increased.

Before pollution . . . More silvery moths could hide from birds and survive to pass on their characteristics.

After pollution . . . More black moths could hide from birds and survive to pass on their characteristics.

The puzzle of the banded snails

The different colours and patterns on the shells of banded snails are affected by the colour of their surroundings, the climate and the behaviour of the birds that eat them. One or more of these natural factors may "select" which snails survive in any one place. But in some places there doesn't seem to be any reason for the huge variety in shell colour and pattern.

This example shows how complicated natural selection is.

Light-shelled snails reflect heat, so survive better in hot places.

Birds are less likely to find snails that match their surroundings.

Birds may learn to recognize the most common shell pattern as their usual food. So out-of-the-ordinary snails are more likely to survive.

Dark-shelled snails absorb more heat, so survive better in cold conditions.

Working in different ways

Sometimes natural selection allows a number of different forms of the same species to exist in a population at the same time.

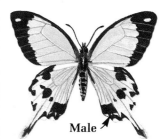

Male

Male mocker swallowtail butterflies all look the same (probably to help females recognize them during courtship).

Female

Disguised females

But there are at least four types of female. One looks like the male. The others each look like a different species of butterfly which taste unpleasant. The three disguises above probably help to protect the females from being eaten by birds while they mate and lay their eggs. The male does not need this sort of protection.

More about Darwin's ideas

According to the theory of natural selection, animals should evolve features that help them to survive and reproduce. So why does the peacock have such a ridiculous tail? . . . and why do deer have antlers? Darwin argued that features such as these probably evolved to help animals compete for a mate.

Sexual selection

Darwin called his idea sexual selection. The features that helped to win a mate would be passed on from generation to generation, with other animals doing the "selecting" instead of the environment.

Sexual selection mostly works in two ways: competition and choice. In some species, males have to compete with each other to win females; in other species, females seem to choose which male they will mate with, as shown in the pictures on this page.

Animal behaviour

The way in which animals behave affects their chances of survival. Why, therefore, do some animals seem to help others, sometimes at their own expense? According to the theory of natural selection, their helpful behaviour is less likely to be passed on, because animals that help others reduce their own chances of survival.

The answer may be that they are really behaving selfishly by helping their relatives, and so making sure that some of their own offspring or relatives survive to pass on their characteristics. They may also know that they are likely to be paid back later. Or they may be gaining food, experience and protection while they wait for the chance to set up on their own.

How males compete for a mate

Males compete either to gain areas to which females are attracted (such as good places to breed or nest, or where there is plenty of food), or to win direct possession of the females themselves.

Males often try to frighten each other away just by using threatening behaviour. If they do fight, they risk injury or even loss of the females to a third male.

In some species, such as dung flies, the male guards the female after mating, to make sure it is his sperm which fertilizes her eggs. His behaviour prevents other males from mating with her until she has laid her eggs.

Male dung fly holding on to a female. He is kicking out to prevent another male from mating with her.

How females choose a mate

Where females do the selecting, the males have developed various means of making themselves more attractive. Here are some examples.

Leaves stripped off branch

▶ Some birds, such as this blue bird of paradise, use their amazing feathers in spectacular displays to attract females. They even strip the leaves and twigs off the branches, so the females will get a better view.

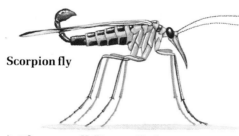

Scorpion fly

◀ Male scorpion flies give their females food (usually an insect) during courtship. Females choose to mate with the males that give them larger-sized insects. They use the protein from their insect gift to lay more eggs.

▶ These small flies, called drosophila, go through a rapid courtship dance before mating. Females are more likely to mate with males that can keep up with them during the last part of this dance. This probably allows them to choose the fittest males as mates.

Drosophila

◀ Male African weaverbirds build nests by weaving strips of leaves into a big hollow ball. Females are more attracted to males with freshly-built green nests than to those with old brown nests.

A newly-built nest

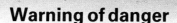

Give and take

Some animals receive help in return for the help they give others (called mutualism or symbiosis). Such animals are more likely to survive together and pass on their helpful behaviour.

For example, cleaner fish pick the parasites off the surface of larger fish. The large fish benefit by getting rid of their parasites and the cleaner fish get a reliable supply of food. Here a wrasse is cleaning a goatfish.

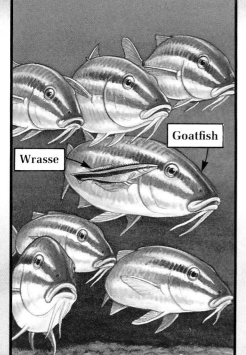

Goatfish

Wrasse

Warning of danger

Some birds and mammals give alarm calls or warning signals if they are in danger. They may be risking their lives to save their fellows. Or they may have selfish reasons for behaving like this.

Springboks leap up and down in this strange way if they spot danger. They may be warning other members of the herd, so that all the herd can escape. Or they may be saying, "Look how fit I am, go after someone else."

How lions help each other

Lions have a complex social life, in which males and females sometimes seem to help each other at their own expense.

The male lions are often related, and help each other to win and defend a pride of lionesses. To avoid injury, or perhaps simply to help a relative, one male may let another mate with a lioness without putting up a fight.

The lionesses are usually related to each other (but not to the males). They help each other to hunt and to look after the cubs. Sharing out the work may help them to survive.

If new males take over the group, they often kill the cubs. The lionesses do not stop them; they may gain more from having cubs with the new males, than by trying to save existing cubs.

The chemical code of life

Darwin worked out his theory of natural selection without knowing how plants and animals are able to produce offspring that are like themselves. He did not know about the chemical code of instructions, called DNA, which is inside the cells of every living thing. But are the offspring exactly the same as their parents? You can begin to see how plants and animals might change and evolve over a long period of time, if you understand how they can change from one generation to the next.

The DNA code of instructions controls the way plants and animals look and the way their bodies work. When plants and animals reproduce, a copy of the instructions is passed on from parents to their offspring. Sometimes these instructions are mixed up, or the code isn't copied exactly, which can lead to change.

Where is the DNA?

All living things are made up of cells. Inside each cell is a nucleus, and inside the nucleus are structures called chromosomes. Each chromosome is made up of sections of DNA, called genes, which instruct the cell what to do. Apart from a few viruses, all living things use DNA, which suggest that all life on Earth might have evolved from the same source.

You are different from a fly or a buttercup because your basic set of instructions, or code, is different from theirs. Different Species can also have different numbers of chromosomes: for example, you have 46, a horse has 63 and some butterflies have 400.

All the cells in a plant or animal contain the full DNA code for that species. But each cell only uses the parts of the code it needs for the job it has to do. It is not yet understood exactly how this process works.

All living things have DNA.

Copying the code

New cells are needed all the time – about 500 million of your body cells die each day and have to be replaced. Every time a new cell is made, the DNA is copied, so that when the cell divides, each of the two new cells has its own copy of the code.

1. The two DNA strands separate.

2. Spare bases are always present and these join up with their matching pairs on the separated strands.

3. Two new strands are formed.

How does the code work

The code spells out different words which are built up into sentences. Each sentence is a gene. There are also codes for stop and start. You can see how this works below.

1. DNA consists of two thin strands wound round each other like a spiral staircase.

2. The steps of the staircase are made up of four chemical building blocks (called bases), which are linked in pairs.

3. The bases can only pair up in a certain way: adenine (letter A) with thymine (T): and guanine (G) with cytosine (C).

4. The bases are like a four-letter alphabet and the letters are read in groups of three. Each group of three letters forms a word.

What does the code do?

The code tells the cell to produce different proteins, which control how your body grows and develops. Your body contains at least 10,000 kinds of proteins.

Proteins are made up of chains of substances called amino acids. Each word codes for a particular type of amino acid. The amino acids are then arranged in the order of the words in each gene. There may be hundreds or thousands of amino acids in each protein chain.

Spare base

Passing on the code

Once the DNA has been copied, the cell is ready to divide and pass on the code. There are two kinds of cell division.

1 The process that creates new cells when you grow, and replaces worn-out cells, is called mitosis. After the DNA has been copied, the cell divides, and the two new cells look the same as the original cell – they each have the same number of chromosomes (which carry the DNA). Only two chromosomes are shown here, to make it easier to understand.

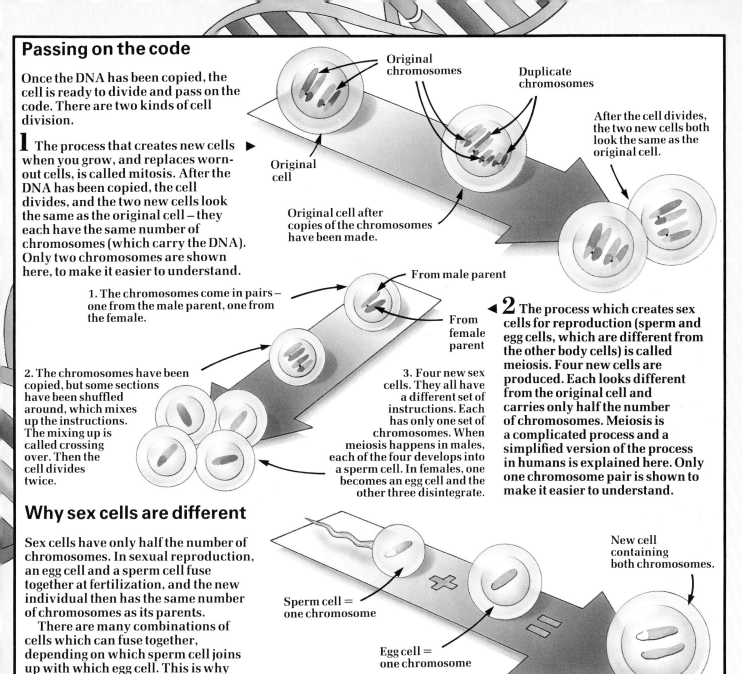

Original
chromosomes

Duplicate
chromosomes

Original
cell

After the cell divides, the two new cells both look the same as the original cell.

Original cell after copies of the chromosomes have been made.

From male parent

From female parent

1. The chromosomes come in pairs – one from the male parent, one from the female.

2. The chromosomes have been copied, but some sections have been shuffled around, which mixes up the instructions. The mixing up is called crossing over. Then the cell divides twice.

3. Four new sex cells. They all have a different set of instructions. Each has only one set of chromosomes. When meiosis happens in males, each of the four develops into a sperm cell. In females, one becomes an egg cell and the other three disintegrate.

◀2 The process which creates sex cells for reproduction (sperm and egg cells, which are different from the other body cells) is called meiosis. Four new cells are produced. Each looks different from the original cell and carries only half the number of chromosomes. Meiosis is a complicated process and a simplified version of the process in humans is explained here. Only one chromosome pair is shown to make it easier to understand.

Why sex cells are different

Sex cells have only half the number of chromosomes. In sexual reproduction, an egg cell and a sperm cell fuse together at fertilization, and the new individual then has the same number of chromosomes as its parents.

There are many combinations of cells which can fuse together, depending on which sperm cell joins up with which egg cell. This is why there is variety between different members of the same species.

Sperm cell = one chromosome

Egg cell = one chromosome

New cell containing both chromosomes.

Making mistakes – mutations

Turn over to see how the genes work

This white tigress is an example of a mutation – she has no gene to make coloured stripes.

Sickle cell anaemia is a blood disease caused by a mistake in just one letter of the DNA code.

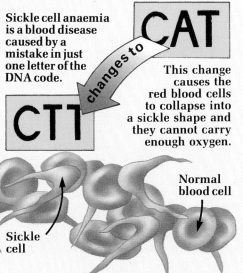

CAT

changes to

CTT

This change causes the red blood cells to collapse into a sickle shape and they cannot carry enough oxygen.

Normal blood cell

Sickle cell

Mistakes (called mutations) sometimes happen to the code. The bases in the DNA might not be copied exactly, or something might go wrong during crossing over in meiosis (see above). The mutation might have the effect that a different protein is made, which could alter the characteristics of its bearer. If mutations occur in the sex cells, they will be passed on and could provide the raw material for the evolution of new species over time.

Most mutations have only a slight effect, or even none at all, if the change does not alter the protein instruction. But some changes can be harmful, or even lethal, because they upset a life process.

The chemical code in action

When plants and animals reproduce, they pass on their genetic code of instructions (including any change to the code) to their offspring. This is called inheritance. A minority of plants and animals inherit an exact copy of the instructions from just one parent and all the offspring have identical sets of genes (called asexual reproduction). The majority inherit a mixture of the genetic instructions from two parents (called sexual reproduction, see page 11), and each offspring has a slightly different set of genes.

The way in which plants and animals then develop depends partly on their inheritance and partly on the conditions in which they live (their environment). The environment affects the way plants and animals grow up, but it does not affect the DNA code.

The different genes which make up the code control your "characteristics", that is, the way you look, how your body works and how you behave. The way genes do this is very complex and is not yet fully understood. But you can find out how some genes work on the page opposite.

The theory of inheritance

During the last century, Gregor Mendel experimented with breeding pea plants to discover how characteristics such as height, seed shape and flower colour were inherited. He kept careful records of the plants he used and the sort of offspring they produced. After many years he worked out his theory of inheritance. Mendel first published his work in 1866, but the significance of his results and ideas was not recognized for nearly 40 years.

Mendel knew nothing about DNA, but his theory – which applies to all living things, including humans – has formed the basis of all studies in genetics. This example of his theory uses the flower colour of peas.

1 For each characteristic, at least one gene is inherited from each parent.

2 Each gene exists in two forms – dominant and recessive. Either one or the other form is inherited from each parent.

3 For each characteristic, the dominant form will appear in the offspring, unless two recessive genes are inherited.

4 The way dominant or recessive genes are inherited depends largely on chance. Mendel worked out that, on average, ¾ inherit at least one dominant gene, and ¼ inherit two recessive genes.

Parent plant with only purple genes

Parent plant with only white genes

Purple is the dominant gene, white is the recessive gene. All offspring will be purple, because they can only inherit one recessive gene.

Parent plants each have one purple gene and one white gene.

Three flowers are purple, one is white – the ratio which Mendel worked out.

The hidden genes
The way a plant or animal looks (called its phenotype) may differ from its genetic make-up (called its genotype). For example, two of the purple flowers shown here carry the recessive gene for white, which they can pass on to their offspring.

Genes and the environment

The environment cannot change the genetic code, but it does affect how the instructions are carried out in an individual.

Two cuttings from one parent plant (which therefore have the same DNA) grown in different environments will look different. But seeds then taken from these cuttings, and grown in the same environment, will produce similar offspring.

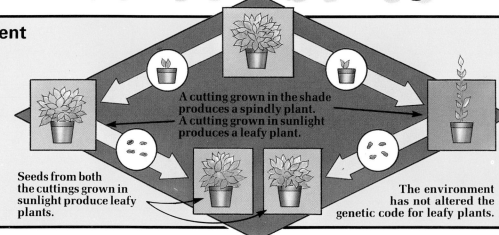

A cutting grown in the shade produces a spindly plant. A cutting grown in sunlight produces a leafy plant.

Seeds from both the cuttings grown in sunlight produce leafy plants.

The environment has not altered the genetic code for leafy plants.

Genes in action

Since Mendel's time, scientists have discovered that very few characteristics are controlled by genes in such a straightforward way as flower colour in peas. For example, genes can exist in more than two forms (as in blood groups, shown on the right). Many characteristics are controlled by more than one gene, whilst some genes seem to switch other genes on and off. If a change is made to a "control" gene, it might affect the way several genes interact with each other, and could lead to a change in characteristics.

Here are a few examples of genes in action in humans, to give you some idea of how complicated the process is.

Blood group AB

Blood group A

Children's genotypes

Parents' genotypes

Blood group B

Blood group O

Boy or girl?

Your sex is controlled by the way the sex chromosomes pair up during fertilization. In humans, each cell has 46 chromosomes, two of which are sex chromosomes. The sex cells have half this amount (see page 11) – 22 plus 1 sex chromosome. Eggs always have an X sex chromosome, sperm have either X or Y. These can pair up as shown on the right, which means that in humans the male determines the sex of the offspring. (This is not always the case; in birds the female sex cells determine the sex of the offspring.)

Genes and blood groups

Your blood group is controlled by a genetic instruction that occurs in three slightly different forms – A, B and O. You inherit one of these from each parent. A and B instructions are both dominant over O, but A and B are neither dominant nor recessive to each other. This is called incomplete dominance.

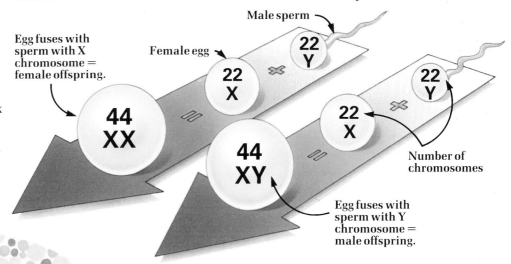

Egg fuses with sperm with X chromosome = female offspring.

Female egg

Male sperm

Number of chromosomes

Egg fuses with sperm with Y chromosome = male offspring.

If you cannot see the difference between red and green . . .

. . . you will not see a teapot here.

Sex-linked genes

Some human characteristics are inherited on the X and Y chromosomes, so it is possible for males and females to inherit different characteristics: for example, the various kinds of colour blindness.

The gene for colour vision occurs only on the X chromosome. If this carries the recessive form of the gene that causes colour blindness, males will be colour blind. Females would have to inherit the recessive gene on both their X chromosomes – which is much less likely -- to be colour blind.

Making an inheritance chart

You could make a family tree showing various characteristics: for example, eye colour, hair colour and height. (Remember to ask older members of the family what colour their hair was when they were young.)

Remember too, for example, that brown eye colour is dominant over blue; dark hair is dominant over fair; and fair hair is dominant over red.

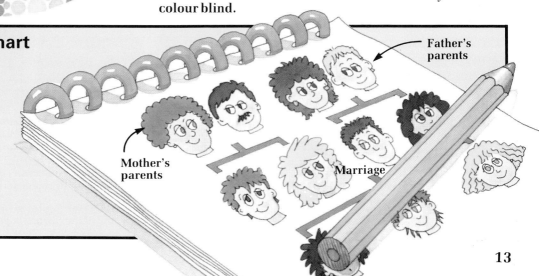

Father's parents

Mother's parents

Marriage

13

What are species?

A species is a group of similar-looking plants or animals that can breed successfully together.[1] The processes of genetic change and natural selection, which you have read about so far, suggest that over long periods of time new species might be formed.

Often, new species evolve when an existing species becomes separated into one or more groups. Each group will have organisms possessing a slightly different set of genes. The differing environments of the two groups will favour (select) different genes, so the organisms become different and will eventually no longer able to breed together.

By looking at the reasons why living species are unable to breed together, it is possible to find out how new species might have been formed in the past and might still be being formed today. Laboratory experiments can provide valuable information about the genetic make-up of different species. One unusual way in which new species can form is called polyploidy (see opposite). This can lead to the "instant" formation of new species – mostly of plants – in only one or two generations.

Genetic drift

There is also the possibility of evolution by chance rather than by natural selection. This is called "genetic drift". It is most likely to be important if a very small group breaks away from the main species.

In the small group, the set of genes is much smaller, and it is a matter of chance which genes have been included. It is possible that one or more genes may be lost entirely. There is also a greater chance of any mutation (good or bad) being passed on, since there is less choice of genes in the group as a whole.

How species form in different areas

Darwin illustrated his ideas about species by his study of life on the Galapagos Islands,[2] where there are 13 species of finches found nowhere else. Each has a different shape or size of beak, eats different food and lives in different surroundings. These are five examples of the finch species.

Large ground finch. Blunt, powerful beak for breaking open large seeds. Lives on coasts and lowlands, mainly at ground level.

Vegetarian tree finch. Eats fruits, buds and seeds. Lives in forests.

Warbler finch. Small pointed beak for probing into cracks. Eats only insects. Lives in forests.

Small tree finch. Strong sharp beak for grabbing and cutting. Eats mainly insects. Lives in trees.

Woodpecker finch. Uses cactus spines as tool to fish insects out of cracks in tree bark.

These finches probably evolved from one species that flew to the islands from the mainland. There were few other bird species on the islands, so the finches took advantage of and adapted to a variety of habitats, that is different surroundings, such as lowlands and forests. The finches are all so different now that none of the species can breed with another.

How species form in the same area

A species may split into two, even when all the individuals live in the same area. For example, one of the types of fruit flies which live in N. America.

Hawthorn   Apple

1. At one time, the flies lived on hawthorn bushes, laid their eggs in August and the maggots hatched in October and ate the ripe fruit.
2. Then apple trees were introduced. Their fruit ripens in September. Perhaps some flies already laid eggs earlier (in July) and the maggots hatched earlier and ate the ripe apples.
3. Gradually, more flies followed the "apple cycle". Both flies still look the same but can be regarded as different species. They can no longer breed together, because they now lay eggs at different times.

1. See page 16 for more about species. 2. Near the Equator, off the west coast of S. America.

Instant species

Under certain conditions, two different species can sometimes breed together: their offspring are called hybrids. These are usually sterile (they cannot reproduce), because they inherit a different set of chromosomes from each parent, which cannot pair up during meiosis (see page 11).

Occasionally, however, the number of chromosomes in the cell is doubled (that is, they are copied but not divided into two cells, see page 11). If the hybrid fertilizes itself (this mostly happens in plants), the chromosomes can pair up, and a "polyploid" will result.

Polyploids *are* able to reproduce, and a new species can then build up over one or two generations.

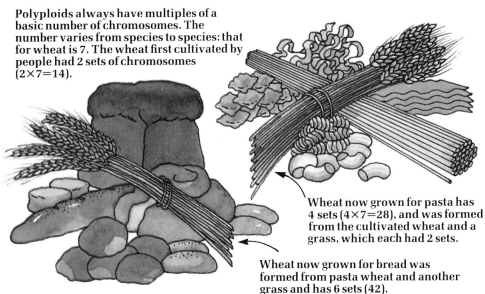

Polyploids always have multiples of a basic number of chromosomes. The number varies from species to species: that for wheat is 7. The wheat first cultivated by people had 2 sets of chromosomes ($2 \times 7 = 14$).

Wheat now grown for pasta has 4 sets ($4 \times 7 = 28$), and was formed from the cultivated wheat and a grass, which each had 2 sets.

Wheat now grown for bread was formed from pasta wheat and another grass and has 6 sets (42).

What keeps living things apart?

Here you can see some examples of living species which can no longer breed together, and the reasons for this. New species usually take a long time to form, so studying living species may provide clues as to how they were formed in the past.

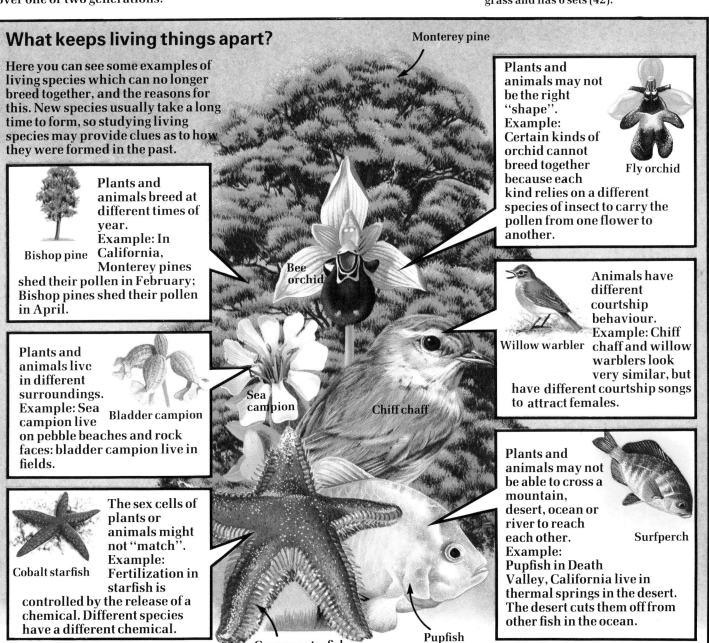

Monterey pine

Plants and animals breed at different times of year.
Example: In California, Monterey pines shed their pollen in February; Bishop pines shed their pollen in April.

Bishop pine

Plants and animals live in different surroundings. Example: Sea campion live on pebble beaches and rock faces: bladder campion live in fields.

Bladder campion

The sex cells of plants or animals might not "match". Example: Fertilization in starfish is controlled by the release of a chemical. Different species have a different chemical.

Cobalt starfish

Plants and animals may not be the right "shape". Example: Certain kinds of orchid cannot breed together because each kind relies on a different species of insect to carry the pollen from one flower to another.

Fly orchid

Animals have different courtship behaviour. Example: Chiff chaff and willow warblers look very similar, but have different courtship songs to attract females.

Willow warbler

Plants and animals may not be able to cross a mountain, desert, ocean or river to reach each other. Example: Pupfish in Death Valley, California live in thermal springs in the desert. The desert cuts them off from other fish in the ocean.

Surfperch

Bee orchid

Sea campion

Chiff chaff

Common starfish

Pupfish

Classification

So far, you have read how all forms of life have the same chemical code, and how it works. You have seen various selection processes at work, and how new species can be formed. Here you can see how the enormous number of living species, and those found as fossil remains, can be "classified", that is, grouped together by comparing features they have in common.

This grouping is based on a system worked out by Carl Linnaeus in the 1750s, and arranges plants and animals into larger and larger groups. By comparing similar features between these groups, classification builds up a picture of how all forms of life are related. And shows how different forms of life might have evolved from a common ancestor.

Looking at different features

Plants and animals are sorted into groups by comparing features they have in common. The sorting can be done in various ways, depending on the features being looked at. These are the features most widely used:
- The appearance of plants and animals.
- The skeletons of animals and the flowering parts of plants.
- How plants and animals develop, for example from seeds, eggs, and so on.

Tiger

These two animals look similar, for example, so they can be grouped together.

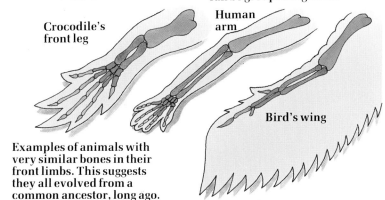

Crocodile's front leg

Human arm

Bird's wing

Examples of animals with very similar bones in their front limbs. This suggests they all evolved from a common ancestor, long ago.

Linnaeus' system of classification

The groups are classified according to Carl Linnaeus' system. Starting with the smallest, he called them: species, genus (pl. genera), family, order, class, phylum (pl. phyla) and kingdom. Here is an example, which shows that a tiger is a flesh-eating mammal with a backbone, belonging to the cat family.

Linnaeus' groups	Subdivision	Meaning of subdivision
Kingdom	Animal	
Phylum	Chordate	Nerve chord running down back
Sub-phylum	Vertebrate	Having a backbone
Class	Mammal	Covered in hair; young feed on mother's milk
Order	Carnivora	Flesh-eating
Family	Felidae	Cats
Genus	*Panthera*	Big cats
Species*	*Panthera tigris*	Tiger

*Species have two-part names which are always written in Latin. The first part gives the genus; the second part the species.

Cladistics

In this method of classification, organisms are grouped into "clades", according to features they all share, but which others do not. For example, a starling is a bird because it has feathers, a feature shared by no other animals. So, birds form a clade.

Similarly, a cow is a mammal because it has mammary glands. All mammals feed their young with milk from mammary glands, a feature shared by no other animals. So mammals form a clade.

Here is a list of animals to be arranged into a group: mouse, starling, cow, goldfish, penguin.

1. The first stage is to identify any shared features:

FEATURE	MOUSE	STARLING	COW	GOLDFISH	PENGUIN
MAMMARY GLAND	✓		✓		
LUNGS	✓	✓	✓		✓
JAWS	✓	✓	✓	✓	✓
FEATHERS		✓			✓

2. The animals are then grouped according to the shared features:

Mouse Cow — Mammary glands
Starling Penguin — Feathers
Goldfish
Lungs
Jaws

3. Finally, a branching diagram, or "cladogram", is drawn:

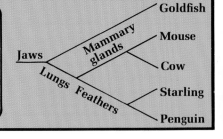

Goldfish
Mouse
Cow
Starling
Penguin

Jaws
Mammary glands
Lungs
Feathers

The origin of life

The beginning of life on Earth is a mystery that has puzzled people for centuries. On this page, you can read about people's early ideas as to the origin of life on Earth.

The most widely accepted scientific theory as to how life began is shown on page 18. There are other theories, one of which – that life may have arrived from outer space – is described below.

Creation stories

People have always imagined how the world might have begun. The first peoples often had similar ideas – regardless of where they lived – partly because they based their stories on what happened in their own lives.

Ancient Egyptian ideas

For example, one Egyptian myth says the world was originally filled with water, from which a hill arose. On the hill a lotus flower grew, and from it emerged the young sun god who created other gods, the land and all creatures. This "happened" to the Ancient Egyptians every year. The River Nile flooded and, as the water went down, the land reappeared and with it the birth of new things.

"Birth" ideas

Many of the ideas are concerned with birth, such as the world being born out of an egg, or out of the body of a dead monster. Other ideas were similar to the Egyptian one described above, although sometimes the gods themselves actually became the world. Other beliefs are concerned with a god (or gods) "speaking" and the world being created, as in the Genesis story.

Aborigine ideas

For the Australian Aborigines, the earth and sky have always existed. But in ancient times (Dreamtime), so one of their stories goes, beings moved over the Earth and their actions and footprints became the landscape – hills, caves, trees, and so on – and all Aborigines were descended from these ancestral beings.

This picture, based on ▶ an Aboriginal bark painting, shows two spirit beings in the form of humans.

Creationism

Creationism is the belief that God created every living thing, each with its own purpose, although not everyone believes it happened exactly as the Bible says.

You can read about three of the various Creationist beliefs below. In each, God is thought to have created "Man", fully developed and intelligent, by a separate act. Creationists do not think that humans evolved from apes. You can also read about the story of Genesis, as told in the Bible.

Genesis story

The story of Genesis in the Bible tells how God spoke, and so created the world in six days.

Light was created – day and night

Day 1

Day 2

The heavens above, the waters beneath

Day 3

The Earth and all green things – the plants and trees

Day 4

Sun, Moon and stars, to divide day from night

Day 5

All living creatures on Earth – and Adam and Eve

Day 6

Birds in the sky, and fish in the sea

Creationist beliefs

● God created the world in exactly six days, as told in Genesis, the first book of the Bible. It happened about 4,004 years before the birth of Jesus Christ.

● God created the world in six "days", each of which lasted for thousands of years. Everything that God had created was destroyed by the Biblical Flood (as shown by the fossil remains). God then re-created the Earth as it is today.

● God has created new forms of life at different times (which is why the fossil record seems incomplete), with small-scale evolution happening in between.

Life from outer space

A few people think the Earth's early atmosphere was too hot for the formation of life. But cells might have been formed in the cold depths of outer space, where there are clouds of dust and gas containing many of the raw materials of life. These cells might have made up part of the tails of comets, which are dense masses of gas and dust. As the comets passed close, some cells could have reached Earth where, by chance process, they might have been "assembled" into life forms.

However, if there are any living cells in outer space, most scientists think that they are unlikely to be able to survive in the very different conditions on Earth.

How life began

The scientific theory of the origin of life is based on experiments which recreate the early atmosphere on Earth, and also on the study of simple life forms alive today. Because all forms of life have the same basic chemistry and genetic code, it is thought that life probably arose only once, and may have evolved from lifeless matter, that is from the gases in the early atmosphere. Here you can see the stages of how life on Earth may have begun.

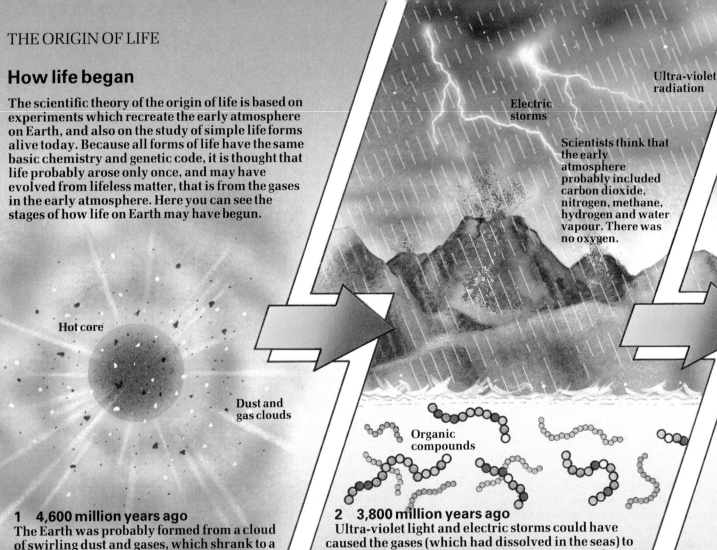

Ultra-violet radiation

Electric storms

Scientists think that the early atmosphere probably included carbon dioxide, nitrogen, methane, hydrogen and water vapour. There was no oxygen.

Hot core

Dust and gas clouds

Organic compounds

1   4,600 million years ago
The Earth was probably formed from a cloud of swirling dust and gases, which shrank to a very hot core. Gradually, the Earth cooled and the first layers of rock were formed. The steam from volcanoes condensed to make rains which created the seas.

2   3,800 million years ago
Ultra-violet light and electric storms could have caused the gases (which had dissolved in the seas) to react and produce a variety of organic compounds. These included amino acids (which might have built up into primitive proteins) and the four bases of DNA (see page 10).

Early forms of life

The earliest record of prokaryotes dates back over 3,000 million years, 1,500 million years before the first record of eukaryotes. In spite of this vast amount of time, it is difficult to see how eukaryotes evolved from prokaryotes. One theory is that the "organelles" (small organs) inside each eukaryotic cell were once different types of prokaryotes which were absorbed (taken in) by other cells. Both prokaryotes and eukaryotes contain DNA, but how the DNA code itself evolved is still not known.

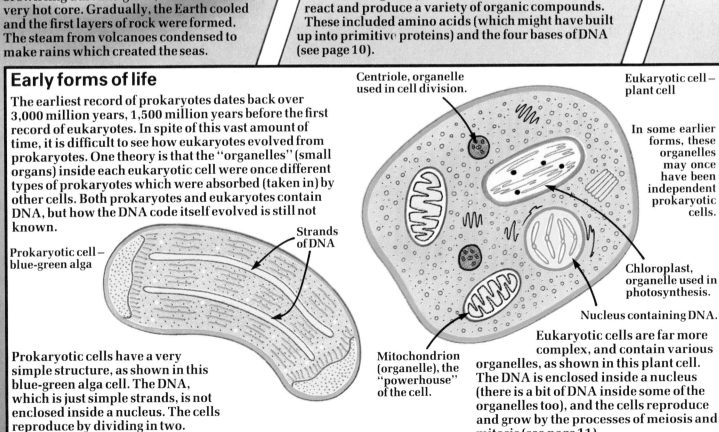

Centriole, organelle used in cell division.

Eukaryotic cell – plant cell

In some earlier forms, these organelles may once have been independent prokaryotic cells.

Strands of DNA

Prokaryotic cell – blue-green alga

Chloroplast, organelle used in photosynthesis.

Mitochondrion (organelle), the "powerhouse" of the cell.

Nucleus containing DNA.

Prokaryotic cells have a very simple structure, as shown in this blue-green alga cell. The DNA, which is just simple strands, is not enclosed inside a nucleus. The cells reproduce by dividing in two.

Eukaryotic cells are far more complex, and contain various organelles, as shown in this plant cell. The DNA is enclosed inside a nucleus (there is a bit of DNA inside some of the organelles too), and the cells reproduce and grow by the processes of meiosis and mitosis (see page 11).

The oxygen formed a protective layer of ozone high in the atmosphere, which screened out harmful ultra-violet radiation.

Anaerobic bacteria (anaerobic means not needing oxygen).

Aerobic bacteria (aerobic means needing oxygen).

3 3,000 million years ago

Although it is not yet known how, some of these compounds came together to create the earliest forms of life, the prokaryotes. These were minute, single-celled organisms, such as bacteria and blue-green algae. These organisms used hydrogen for photosynthesis (energy production).

4 1,500 million years ago

Some bacteria started to use carbon dioxide and water for photosynthesis, and oxygen was given off as a waste product. The release of oxygen caused a dramatic change. Until then, most life forms had lived under water, for protection from the harmful ultra-violet radiation. Now this radiation was screened out by the oxygen, which formed an ozone layer high in the atmosphere. New, more complex, life forms (called eukaryotes) arose, and gradually a greater variety of life evolved on the surface of and near the edges of the seas. Finally, life started to appear on the land.

The life "clock"

This clock face gives some idea of the amount of time taken for life to evolve. Bacteria did not begin until about 20 minutes past the hour, with the earliest forms of animal life, such as jellyfish and plant life, such as algae, not starting until about ¼ to the hour. The first land plants, and animals such as reptiles and amphibians, arrived between ¼ to and 5 to. The dinosaurs arrived about 3 minutes to; the apes about 40 seconds to the hour. Humans first appeared just as the hour strikes.

Humans, 5 million years ago

Apes, 35 million years ago

Dinosaurs, 200 million years ago

Reptiles, 340 million years ago

570 million years ago

4,600 million years ago

Algae and jellyfish

Plants, 500 million years ago

Bacteria

1,500 million years ago

3,000 million years ago

The fossil record

On the previous page, the life clock shows that the earliest forms of life appeared more than 3,000 million years ago. Evidence for these and other life forms can be seen from the fossilized remains of plants and animals. These have been found in the various layers of rock which have been formed over time, although only a few fossils have been found in the earliest layers – called the Pre-Cambrian layers. The fossil record itself has many gaps, partly because not all plants and animals become fossilized, and partly because it is not possible to find all the fossils "locked" into the rocks. Even so, enough remains have been found to work out a timescale of the evolution of some of the different forms of life.

How rocks are formed

Rocks are constantly being eroded (worn away) by wind, rain and ice. The bits of rock, called sediments, are swept away into lakes and seas by the wind and rain.

The sediments sink to form layers under the water, and are gradually packed down by the weight of new layers on top. Over millions of years, the sediments harden to form layers of rock, called strata. If plant or animal remains are trapped in the sediment, they may become fossilized.

Rocks of different ages are exposed one on top of the other, with the oldest at the bottom.

The different layers of rock are called strata.

The strata have been pushed upwards from the bottom.

Erosion exposes strata of different ages side by side.

This "slice" through the Earth shows that the strata are not always neatly arranged on top of each other. Sometimes movements in the Earth's crust have disturbed them, which can make it difficult to work out the sequence of fossils. Here you can see how movement has forced the strata upwards.

How fossils are formed

Most plants and animal remains are either decomposed (broken down) by bacteria and fungi or eaten by animals. Plants and animals become fossilized only if they are buried fairly quickly, that is, covered by drifting sand or drowned in mud and silt. These conditions do not exist everywhere, which is why only a small proportion of plants and animals become fossilized.

Here are three examples of how fossils can be formed.

The impression left behind by a brittlestar, after it decayed away.

"Trace" fossils can sometimes be preserved, if impressions have been left by decayed matter – such as leaf imprints, worm trails and even dinosaur footprints – or "moulds" of shells which have dissolved away.

When plants and animals die, the "soft" parts usually rot away, so most fossil remains are the "hard" parts, for example, shells, teeth, bone and wood. Over time, these can be preserved by minerals being formed within them.

Ammonite shells preserved by the formation of minerals.

An ant preserved in amber (hardened resin).

Very occasionally, the soft parts of remains are preserved. Such fossils are usually found in the most recent strata.

Continental drift

The continents have not always been in the same position on the globe as they are today. For example, this is probably how the globe looked 200 million years ago.

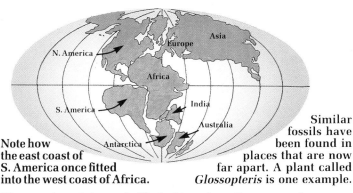

Note how the east coast of S. America once fitted into the west coast of Africa.

Similar fossils have been found in places that are now far apart. A plant called *Glossopteris* is one example.

The continents have drifted. At various times, seas have covered land which is now mountains, and the climate has changed greatly over time (for example, Africa was once covered in ice). This is why fossil remains have been found where, today, similar plants and animals could not survive.

How continental drift works

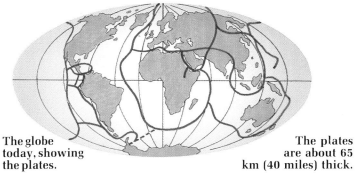

The globe today, showing the plates.

The plates are about 65 km (40 miles) thick.

The Earth's outer layer is divided into sections called plates, which drift past each other at the rate of about 2 cm (½ in) a year. Where plates are moving apart, new hot molten (liquid) rock rises up from inside the Earth to "plug the gap". Where plates meet, one slides down under the other. All this causes pressure inside the Earth, which is one reason for the movement, such as folding, of the strata.

Pre-Cambrian fossils

The first life forms date back to the Pre-Cambrian strata, over 3,000 million years ago. Very few fossils have been found, partly because the creatures were mostly soft-bodied.

From the Cambrian strata onwards, far more fossil remains have been found, and it is possible to picture how life might have looked, as shown on pages 22-25. Not all the plants and creatures shown existed at the same time and in the same place.

These are examples of Pre-Cambrian trace fossils.

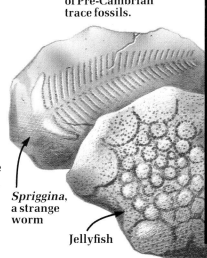

Spriggina, a strange worm

Jellyfish

Timechart of life on Earth

This "cliff" shows the names of the various strata and how long ago they were formed. (The Pre-Cambrian strata covers so many millions of years that it is not possible to include it on these pages.) The strata is divided into eras as shown: Palaeozic (ancient life), Mesozoic (middle life) and Cenozoic (new life).

	million years ago		
Cenozoic		Today	
	0.01	Holocene	Modern humans
	2	Pleistocene	Early humans
	5	Pliocene	"Ape-people"
	22	Miocene	Grazing animals
			Early apes
	38	Oligocene	Modern mammals
			Early elephants
	55	Eocene	Early horses
	65	Palaeocene	
Mesozoic	140	Cretaceous	Flowering plants Small mammals
	195	Jurassic	Dinosaurs
	230	Triassic	Large reptiles Birds, snakes and lizards
Palaeozic	280	Permian	
	345	Carboniferous	Plant-eating reptiles
	395	Devonian	Amphibians
	435	Silurian	Land vertebrates Insects
	500	Ordovician	Land plants Fungi Vertebrates with jaws
	570	Cambrian	Jawless vertebrates Molluscs Crustaceans Echinoderms
			Worms Jellyfish, etc.
	3,500	Pre-Cambrian	Bacteria Blue-green algae

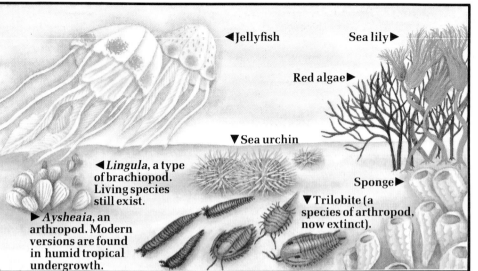

Cambrian
570-500 million years ago

The variety of life forms seems to have exploded at the beginning of the Cambrian Period. Life forms were still only to be found in the seas, but the earlier forms now evolved into a variety of invertebrate forms (that is, creatures without backbones), including:

– Brachiopods (hinged shells, fixed to the seabed by a foot).
– Arthropods ("shelled" creatures), such as trilobites, relatives of modern insects, spiders, lobsters and crabs.
– Echinoderms (spiny-skinned) creatures, such as sea urchins.

◀Jellyfish   Sea lily▶

Red algae▶

▼Sea urchin

◀*Lingula*, a type of brachiopod. Living species still exist.

Sponge▶

▶*Aysheaia*, an arthropod. Modern versions are found in humid tropical undergrowth.

▼Trilobite (a species of arthropod, now extinct).

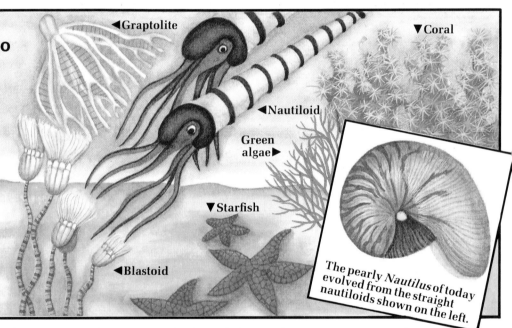

Ordovician
500-435 million years ago

Life forms still remained in the sea, but the creatures became larger in size, and diversified still further, including:

– Cephalopods such as octopus, nautiloids (which later evolved into ammonites) and squid. These were some of the first creatures that could swim; most of the earlier life forms were fixed to or could only move about on the seabed.
– Vertebrates (creatures with backbones), for example jawless fish covered with bony armour.

◀Graptolite   ▼Coral

◀Nautiloid

Green algae▶

▼Starfish

◀Blastoid

The pearly *Nautilus* of today evolved from the straight nautiloids shown on the left.

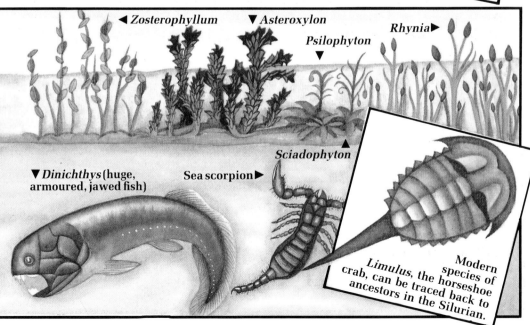

Silurian
435-395 million years ago

By the end of the Silurian Period, life had at last appeared on land.
– Marsh plants started to grow at the edges of the sea (they needed to be near water to reproduce). They probably evolved from the algae which started to grow in the Cambrian Period.
– Giant arthropods (sea scorpions) moved onto the seashore.

◀*Zosterophyllum*   ▼*Asteroxylon*   *Rhynia*▶

Psilophyton
▼

Sciadophyton

▼*Dinichthys* (huge, armoured, jawed fish)   Sea scorpion▶

Modern species of *Limulus*, the horseshoe crab, can be traced back to ancestors in the Silurian.

Devonian
394-345 million years ago

The Devonian Period is known as the "Age of Fishes". Plant life also expanded in the swamps and marshes.

– Fish developed bony skeletons and swim bladders (the earliest form of lung). Some fish developed paired fins, which eventually enabled them to "walk" onto land, where their "lungs" helped them to survive out of water.
– Sharks began to develop.
– The first amphibians (cold-blooded vertebrates) evolved from the "lunged" fish. They had to stay near water, in order to keep their bodies moist and to be able to breed.
– The first insects probably appeared.
– Trees and forests began to form.

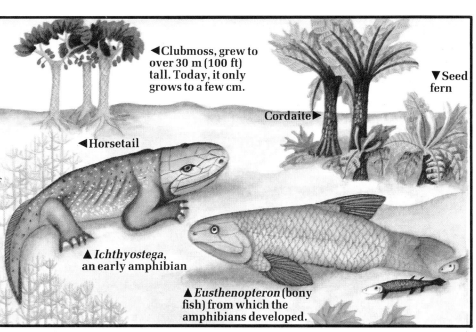

◄Clubmoss, grew to over 30 m (100 ft) tall. Today, it only grows to a few cm.

▼Seed fern

Cordaite►

◄Horsetail

▲*Ichthyostega*, an early amphibian

▲*Eusthenopteron* (bony fish) from which the amphibians developed.

Carboniferous
345-280 million years ago

The climate started to become much drier. Gymnosperm (non-flowering, seed-bearing) plants developed, as did a greater variety of insect and animal life. What we now dig up as coal was formed at this time. (Coal is decayed plant life, fossilized in the swampy sediments.)

– Conifer (cone-bearing) trees first appeared.
– The first reptiles evolved from amphibians. They laid hard-shelled eggs and had dry, scaly skin to retain their body moisture. Therefore, they did not need to stay near water in order to survive. They were herbivores (plant eaters) and, in the Jurassic Period, some developed into warm-blooded mammals.
– Ammonites developed from nautiloids.

►*Meganeura*, giant dragonfly

►Cycad, early palm-type tree (living species are very similar)

▼*Hylonomus*, early reptile

►Lycopod, grew over 30 m (100 ft) tall

◄*Microbrachis*, early amphibian

Permian
280-230 million years ago

The Permian Period saw the swampy primitive forests being replaced by conifer and gingko (Maidenhair) trees. The Appalachian Mountains and many of the deserts were formed. Amphibians and insects were still developing, but it was the reptile group which really started to expand.

– Sail-backed reptiles appeared. (Mammals, including humans, eventually evolved from these creatures.)
– Trilobites became extinct (died out).

Gingko ► tree

▲*Dimetrodon*, sail-backed reptile

▲*Millerosaurus*

▲*Petrolacosaurus*

Triassic
230-195 million years ago

The Triassic marked the beginning of the "Age of the Reptiles". The spread of the gymnosperms continued.
– Conifers, such as firs, pines and cedars, expanded as the horsetails and seed ferns started to die out.
– Palm-like trees started to develop.
– In the sea, the reptiles included turtles; on land, the ancestors of snakes and lizards.
– Ammonites dominated the seas.

Jurassic
195-140 million years ago

During the Jurassic, the climate was warm everywhere – even the Poles had no ice covering – and shallow seas covered much of the land. The cone-bearing plants (such as conifers) dominated the landscape. The first small mammals appeared; but the reptiles, including the dinosaurs, ruled the air, land and sea.
– In the air were reptile-birds, such as *Rhamphorhychus*; on land, some dinosaurs fed on plants, whilst others fed on mammals and smaller dinosaurs.
– Small mammals (warm-blooded vertebrates) were mostly active at night and fed mainly on insects.

Cretaceous
140-65 million years ago

The continents continued to drift apart, and the Rockies and Andes were formed. The first angiosperms (flowering plants) appeared, which provided a new source of food. The mammals developed still further, as did some of the dinosaurs. But, by the end of the Cretaceous, *all* the dinosaurs had become extinct, as had all the ammonites and most of the microscopic plant life in the seas.
– Three main types of mammals had emerged: monotremes (egg-laying, such as the duck-billed platypus), marsupials (pouched, such as the kangaroo) and placentals (from which humans eventually developed).

Rhamphorhychus Jurassic

Brachiosaurus Jurassic

Allosaurus Jurassic

Archaeopteryx Jurassic

Parasaurolophus Cretaceous

Ichthyosaur Triassic

Tyrannosaurus Cretaceous

Palm-type tree Triassic

Pleiosaur Triassic

Stegosaurus Jurassic

Alamosaurus Cretaceous

Ornithomimus Cretaceous

Crocodile Triassic

Ornitholestes Jurassic

Magnolia Cretaceous

Lizard Cretaceous

Turtle Triassic

Early mammal Cretaceous

*Not all the plants and animals shown here were alive at the same time and in the same place.

Palaeocene
65-55 million years ago

During the Palaeocene, the flowering plants dominated the landscape. The extinction of the dinosaurs enabled the mammals to take over – rodents (such as rats and mice), carnivores (such as cats and dogs) and primates (such as monkeys). They were mostly ground-living and no longer needed to live by night. The continued drifting of the continents cut off some groups of mammals from others, such as the marsupials in Australasia.

Eocene and Oligocene
55-22 million years ago

By the start of the Eocene Period, the variety of flowering plants and mammals had further developed, to take advantage of the different habitats and sources of food. The ancestors of elephants and horses appeared. The primates had evolved into "grasping" tree-climbers, where they fed on the leaves, fruit, nuts and sap. They also had better eyesight than earlier mammals, because the position of the eyes in the skull had changed to face the front. The Himalayas and Alps were formed only about now.

Miocene, Pliocene and Pleistocene
22 million-10 thousand years ago

The climate changed dramatically during the Miocene Period. The temperature dropped and grasslands replaced much of the woodlands and forests. This change led to the emergence of herds of grazing animals. The first apes also evolved.

The first hominids (early humans) arrived during the Pliocene Period, the end of which saw the start of the Ice Age. Many mammals died out; but some survived the cold (such as woolly mammoths), whilst others moved south to warmer weather. The Pleistocene Period began after the Ice Age, about two million years ago.

Baluchitherium, early rhino Oligocene

Teratornis, vulture Pleistocene

Deiontherium, early elephant Miocene

Poebrotherium, early camel Oligocene

Brontotherium Oligocene

Macrauchenia Pleistocene

Uintatherium, six-horned herbivore Eocene

Diatryma, flight-less bird Eocene

Megatherium, giant ground sloth Pleistocene

Duck-billed platypus Palaeocene

Echidna (spiny ant-eater) Palaeocene

Hyracotherium (*Eohippus*), earliest horse Eocene

Palaeolagus, early hare Oligocene

Paramys, early rats and mice Eocene

Smilodon, sabre-toothed cat Pleistocene

This page shows some of the ancestors of modern animals.

Turn over to read about human evolution

Human evolution

Were humans brought onto the Earth fully-formed and intelligent, as told in the Bible? Or do humans share an ancestor with apes? Even for those who believe in the second alternative, there are still many theories about the fossil remains of hominids (early humans): one problem is the gap in the fossil record, between 8 and 4 million years ago.

Shown here is a possible version of human evolution. Until more fossil evidence is found, the complete version will remain unknown.

Classifying the apes

Humans are classified into the primate order in the chordate phylum.[1] Primates are a group of animals which includes apes, that is gibbons, orang-utans, gorillas and chimpanzees. The exact relationship between the apes is difficult to work out, since there are arguments as to which features are most important for comparison.

This is one possible classification, comparing features such as size and shape of skull, brain and teeth.

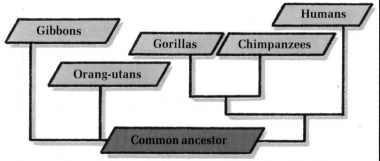

As you can see, humans appear to be more closely related to chimpanzees and gorillas than to the other apes. However, some studies suggest that humans may be more closely related to chimpanzees, while others have indicated that gorillas may be our closest living relatives.

The human element

Although humans are grouped with the apes, they differ greatly, as shown here. But it is by looking for features we share with apes, or with fossil remains, that it may be possible to work out exactly how humans evolved.

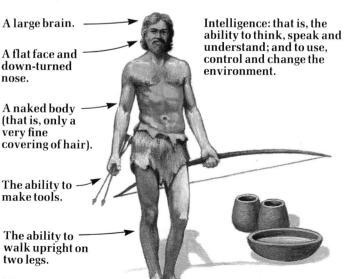

A large brain.

A flat face and down-turned nose.

A naked body (that is, only a very fine covering of hair).

The ability to make tools.

The ability to walk upright on two legs.

Intelligence: that is, the ability to think, speak and understand; and to use, control and change the environment.

The fossil evidence

The map (opposite) shows you where some of the fossil remains have been found. Except for *Ramapithecus* (which is probably not closely related to humans at all), those of earliest date have been found in Africa.

Ramapithecus

The fossil remains are of jaw bones and teeth only, but it is possible that *Ramapithecus* looked like this. Some people now think that they were more closely related to orang-utans than to any of the other apes.

Ramapithecus 14 million years ago was first found in India, and named after *Rama* (a Hindu god) and *pithecus* (the Greek for monkey or ape).

The fossil gap

Fossils have not yet been found for the period between 8-4 million years ago. One possible reason is that much of the land was covered by shallow seas and some apes might have adapted to their new habitat by taking to the water in search of food and shelter. This theory could explain why fossils found after the gap have features which humans do not share with other primates, such as little body hair, a layer of fat under the skin and breath control under water, all of which are helpful when swimming.

Australopithecus ("southern ape")

Evidence of three main species has been found. They walked upright and used bones and stones as tools. However, they shared some features with gorillas and chimpanzees, and this suggests that the split between apes and hominids happened during this period.

Australopithecus afarensis. Parts of a skeleton were found in Hadar, in Ethiopia, and nicknamed "Lucy". This is how she may have looked.

Australopithecus 4 million years ago

Australopithecus gracile

Australopithecus robustus

1. Classification is explained on page 16.

Homo erectus ("upright man")
Homo erectus probably first evolved in Africa and South-East Asia, and then moved northwards to Europe and North Asia. As well as walking upright and using stone tools to make tools, *Homo erectus* used fire for cooking – a feature shared with modern humans but not with *Homo habilis*. So *Homo erectus* is a closer relative of modern humans than *Homo habilis*.

Homo sapiens neanderthalensis
Neandertals lived mostly in Europe and the Middle East before and during the last Ice Age, about 100,000 years ago. Like *Homo erectus*, they walked on two legs, made tools and used fire. But, like modern humans, they had ceremonies and buried their dead. This last feature is shared only with modern humans, so the neandertals are probably more closely related to us than to the *Homo erectus* people.

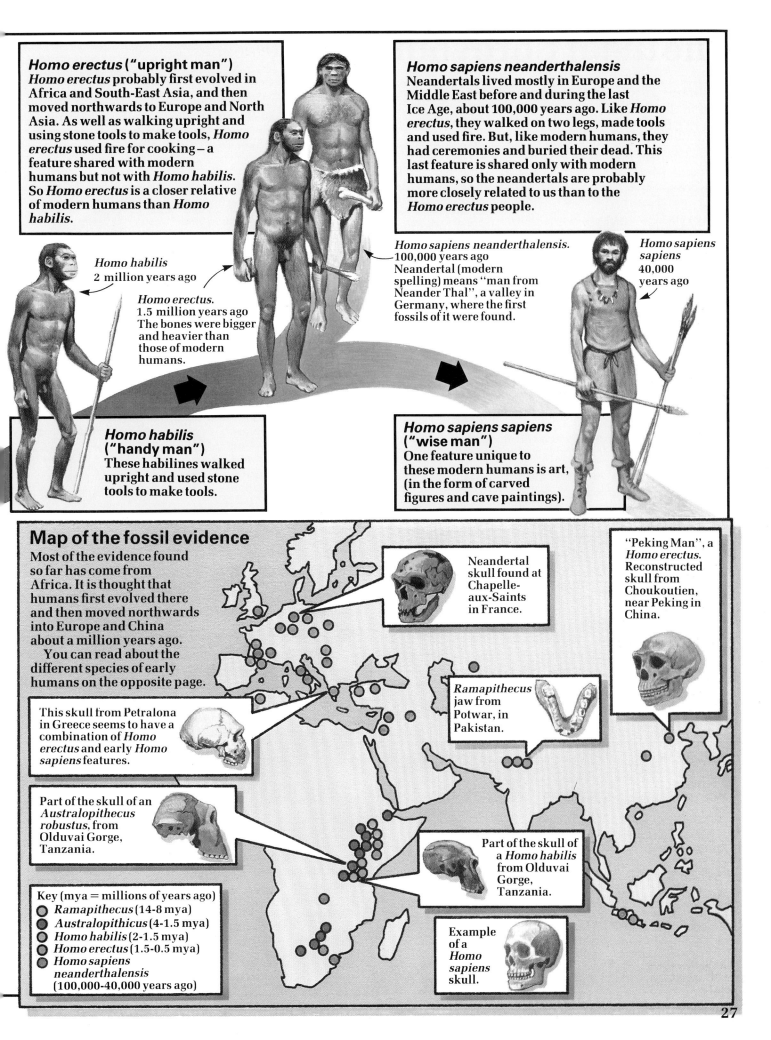

Homo habilis 2 million years ago

Homo erectus. 1.5 million years ago The bones were bigger and heavier than those of modern humans.

Homo sapiens neanderthalensis. 100,000 years ago Neandertal (modern spelling) means "man from Neander Thal", a valley in Germany, where the first fossils of it were found.

Homo sapiens sapiens 40,000 years ago

Homo habilis ("handy man")
These habilines walked upright and used stone tools to make tools.

Homo sapiens sapiens ("wise man")
One feature unique to these modern humans is art, (in the form of carved figures and cave paintings).

Map of the fossil evidence
Most of the evidence found so far has come from Africa. It is thought that humans first evolved there and then moved northwards into Europe and China about a million years ago.

You can read about the different species of early humans on the opposite page.

Neandertal skull found at Chapelle-aux-Saints in France.

"Peking Man", a *Homo erectus*. Reconstructed skull from Choukoutien, near Peking in China.

This skull from Petralona in Greece seems to have a combination of *Homo erectus* and early *Homo sapiens* features.

Ramapithecus jaw from Potwar, in Pakistan.

Part of the skull of an *Australopithecus robustus*, from Olduvai Gorge, Tanzania.

Part of the skull of a *Homo habilis* from Olduvai Gorge, Tanzania.

Key (mya = millions of years ago)
- *Ramapithecus* (14-8 mya)
- *Australopithicus* (4-1.5 mya)
- *Homo habilis* (2-1.5 mya)
- *Homo erectus* (1.5-0.5 mya)
- *Homo sapiens neanderthalensis* (100,000-40,000 years ago)

Example of a *Homo sapiens* skull.

The theory of evolution

The theory of evolution is made up of many ideas, as you have seen in this book. These two pages summarize the ideas, to help you understand how they all fit together.

There are many questions in the story of evolution which scientists have not yet been able to answer definitely, although there are plenty of possible answers. You can read about two of these puzzling questions here. Why are there so many gaps in the fossil record? Why have many different creatures sometimes become extinct at the same time?

The fossil gaps

Darwin's theory of natural selection suggests that, mostly, new species have evolved slowly and gradually. But in the fossil record there are usually jumps between species. Here are some of the theories to explain the gaps.

- Not all the fossils have been found.

- No fossils were formed, because the conditions at the time were not right for the preservation of plant and animal remains.

- New species evolved in isolated groups on the edges of a main group. When the new species eventually took over from the main group – which had stayed the same – the new species seemed to have evolved suddenly.

- New species evolved so rapidly, that the intermediate stages were unlikely to be preserved.

1 All living things are controlled by the same chemical code – DNA – which spells out the genetic instructions for each species. This suggests that all life arose from the same beginning.

Mistakes to the code, which can alter the characteristics of living things, can sometimes be passed on from parents to offspring. This is how life on Earth could have changed over time.

3 The species are classified, by sorting them into larger and larger groups which share some common features. Every species is classified into one of the main groupings: the phyla.

Being able to group species together in this way, supports the idea that all life forms evolved over time from a common ancestor.

These two species look similar, and can be grouped together.

2

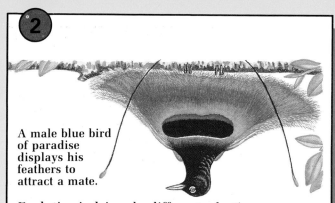

A male blue bird of paradise displays his feathers to attract a mate.

Evolution is driven by different selection processes. Under natural selection, the fittest survive and pass on their genes. In sexual and social selection, this takes the form of competing for and choosing a mate, and how animals behave towards each other.

4 Evidence for many of the species which have existed can be seen from the fossilized remains of plants and animals, which have been trapped during the process of rock formation. This also suggests that life on Earth has evolved over time, as the rock strata, and therefore the fossils inside them, can be dated and arranged in sequence.

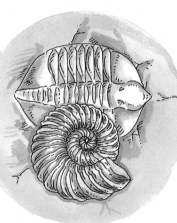

Fossil remains of an ammonite and a trilobite.

Mass extinctions

Throughout time, many individual species have become extinct, as a natural process of evolution. Occasionally, however, there have been mass extinctions, when many kinds of plants and animals have died out at the same time.

At the end of the Cretaceous Period, for example, 65 million years ago, all the dinosaurs suddenly died out, and many other life forms as well, especially those living in the seas. Scientists argue about what caused this, particularly as the extinctions happened to marine as well as land-living creatures. Here are some of their theories.

●Meteorites showered the Earth, causing tidal waves, volcanic eruptions, and clouds of dust and gas which blotted out the Sun's rays.

●The lethal rays from the collapse of a supernova (exploding star) caused a long-term drop in temperature.

●Continental drift may have caused a gradual change in the climate, thus destroying sources of food and shelter.

●The extinctions were not "sudden"; they happened over as long as 500,000 years. Many creatures may already have been in decline, and died out naturally, not as a result of sudden changes.

5 The building blocks of life, that is, organic compounds, first appeared about 3,000 million years ago. This probably resulted from chance reaction between various gases in the atmosphere, ultra-violet radiation and electric storms.

Prokaryote cell.▶ Similar life forms still exist today, such as bacteria.

◀Eukaryote cell. Most life forms – extinct and living – are made up of this type of cell.

About 3,000 million years ago, the compounds came together to create simple forms of life – the prokaryotes, in which DNA is not enclosed inside a nucleus. About 1,500 million years ago, more complex forms of life appeared – the eukaryotes, made up of DNA enclosed inside a nucleus and various organelles.

7 The fossil record shows that millions of species have become extinct during the evolution of life on Earth. They mostly died out due to natural causes, but humans have killed off many species. Humans have also been responsible for the evolution of new kinds of living things. For example, in artificial selection, people have changed plants and animals, by breeding chosen individuals together.

The 110 breeds of dog are the result of artificial selection.

6 Not all species have either evolved or become extinct – some have continued to stay the same for millions of years, often whilst new species have branched off from them. This may be because they are so well-adapted to their habitat, which has also not changed greatly over time.

Limulus, the horseshoe crab. Modern species look the same as those which lived 400 million years ago.

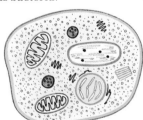

8 The process of evolution took many thousands of millions of years, as shown on the life clock. And the scientific theory of evolution, as described in this book, shows how the amazing variety of life forms on Earth – extinct and living species – could all have evolved from a common origin.

570 million years ago

3,000 million years ago

Who's who

On this page, you can read about a few of the people who have contributed scientific ideas, which have helped towards working out the theory of evolution.

Carl Linnaeus (1707-78), Swedish naturalist. He was the first to try and sort out living things and look for relationships between them. He devised a system for classifying and naming plants and animals.

James Hutton (1726-97), Scottish geologist. He worked out the process of rock formation, and argued that each stratum took many millions of years to form.

Jean Baptiste de Lamarck (1744-1829), French naturalist. One of the first people to suggest that species changed over time and were not fixed, and to suggest evolution as a reason why. However, he is better known for believing that plants and animals could change their characteristics in their own lifetime, and pass these changes on to the next generation.

Sir Charles Lyell (1797-1875), British geologist. He saw that "the present is the key to the past", that is, that the natural forces responsible for creating the world, such as erosion, are still at work now, and that change is a slow, unending process. He called his idea uniformitarianism, and it greatly influenced Charles Darwin.

Charles Darwin (1809-82), British naturalist. As a result of his voyage on HMS *Beagle* (1831-6), and his studies of living and extinct species, he put forward his idea of natural selection to explain evolution. He published his theory in 1859 in his book, *On the Origin of Species*.

Alfred Russel Wallace (1823-1913), British traveller and naturalist. Like Darwin, Wallace also arrived at the theory of natural selection as an explanation of evolution. He sent a copy of his work to Darwin and they published joint details of the theory in 1858. This encouraged Darwin into finally publishing the book he had been working on for 26 years.

Thomas Henry Huxley (1825-95), British zoologist. He defended Darwin's theory of natural selection, and that humans had evolved from apes (both of which were very controversial ideas at the time).

Gregor Mendel (1822-84), a monk born in Silesia in Austria, in what is now part of Czechoslovakia. He experimented with pea plants and worked out that parents can pass on characteristics to their offspring – the theory of inheritance. The importance of his work was not recognized until the beginning of the 20th century.

George Gaylord Simpson (1902-84), American palaeontologist. He studied and classified the evolution of mammals, especially those of S. America. He also showed that the fossil record is compatible with Darwin's theory of natural selection.

Sir Ronald Fisher (1890-1962), British geneticist, **J.B.S. Haldane** (1892-1964), British geneticist and **Sewall Wright** (1889-), American geneticist. In the 1920s, they worked out the "synthetic" theory of evolution, by showing how Darwin's theory of natural selection and Mendel's theory of inheritance work together, through the genes passed on from parents to offspring.

Ernst Mayr (1904-), German-American zoologist. He defended the "geographic" theory of the formation of species, according to which new species are more likely to arise in a group which has been cut off from the main species group.

Francis Crick (1916-), British molecular biologist and **James Watson** (1928-), American biochemist. In 1953, they worked out that the DNA molecule has the form of a double helix, the two spirals of which can unzip, so that the genetic code can be copied.

Stanley Miller (1930-), American chemist. In 1953, he experimented with a mixture of gases which were probably present in the early atmosphere, and showed that intense heat and electric storms could have created a variety of organic compounds, the building blocks of life. (Earlier, in 1924, the Russian, **A.I. Oparin**, had first put forward the idea that life on Earth was formed from non-living matter, that is, from the gases in the early atmosphere.)

Motoo Kimura (1924-), Japanese geneticist. He has argued that evolutionary changes in molecules usually take place by chance rather than by natural selection.

Louis Leakey (1903-72), British anthropologist and his wife **Mary Leakey** (1913-), British palaeoanthropologist, discovered the fossils of early humans at Olduvai Gorge in Tanzania. Their finds showed that early humans had first evolved in Africa (not in Asia, as had previously been thought). Their son, **Richard Leakey** (1943-) has continued their work of looking for evidence of early humans.

William Hamilton (1936-), British biologist. He has developed the theory of "kin selection" to explain why social animals sometimes help one another.

Stephen Jay Gould (1941-), American evolutionary biologist and **Niles Eldredge** (1943-), American palaeobiologist. They think the jumps in the fossil record show long periods with little or no change, interrupted by shorter period when new species arise – usually in small groups living in isolation, and in which favourable mutations can spread more quickly than in a larger group.

Glossary

Amphibians. Vertebrate animals, most of which have to return to water in order to breed; for example, frogs.

Angiosperms. Flowering plants, with seeds enclosed inside a casing, such as a pod.

Annelids. Aquatic or land animals, with soft bodies that are divided into rings or segments; for example, earthworms.

Characteristics. The way an individual looks and behaves, and how its body works.

Chromosomes. Thread-like structures, found in plant and animal cells, which are made of DNA.

Classification. The system of grouping plants and animals, according to features they have in common.

Creationism. The belief that God created the Earth and every living thing, and in particular that He separately created each species, which never change.

DNA. (deoxyribonucleic acid). The DNA molecule carries the genetic code of instructions that controls the characteristics of living things.

Environment. The surroundings in which a plant or animal lives.

Eukaryote cells. Cells which have a nucleus enclosing the DNA.

Evolution. The gradual change in the characteristics of a group of plants or animals over time, which produces new species.

Extinction. The complete loss of a species, that is, all the members of the species die out.

Fertilization. The fusion of an egg cell and a sperm cell to create a new individual.

Fossils. The preserved remains of plants and animals.

Genes. Portions of DNA, each of which carries part of the chemical code of instructions.

Genotype. The genetic make-up of a plant or animal.

Gymnosperms. Non-flowering plants, the seeds of which are not enclosed inside a casing.

Habitat. The particular place in the environment where a plant or animal is usually found; for example, seashore, desert, etc.

Hybrid. The offspring produced when a male and female of different species mate together. Hybrids are mostly sterile, which means that they are usually unable to reproduce.

Invertebrates. Animals without a backbone.

Mammals. Warm-blooded, vertebrate animals, the young of which are fed on their mother's milk.

Marsupials. Pouched mammals; for example, kangaroos.

Meiosis. Cell division to produce sperm and egg cells in animals and pollen and ovules in plants, each with half the number of chromosomes as in the original cell.

Mitosis. Cell division which results in two new cells, each identical to the original cell.

Molecule. The smallest particle of any substance (such as an organic compound), that could exist on its own in nature.

Molluscs. Soft-bodied and unsegmented creatures that are usually covered by a shell; for example, snail.

Mutation. A change in the DNA code, which can sometimes be passed on from parents to offspring.

Natural selection. Theory according to which, the individuals who are best adapted to the environment survive to reproduce and pass on their helpful characteristics to their offspring.

Phyla. The largest groups of the plant and animal kingdoms.

Placentals. Mammals which are nourished (fed) before birth through the placenta in the mother's womb.

Polyploid. An organism (usually a plant) with more than the usual two sets of chromosomes. In hybrids, polyploidy may enable successful reproduction.

Prokaryote cells. Cells in which the DNA is not enclosed inside a nucleus.

Reptiles. Cold-blooded, egg-laying vertebrate animals with scaly skins; for example, crocodiles.

Species. A group of individuals that can successfully breed together.

Vertebrates. Animals with a backbone.

Books to read

The Age of the Earth by John Thackray (Geological Museum, HMSO)

Dinosaurs by Anne McCord (Usborne)

Discovering Genetics by Norman Cohen (Longman)

Discovering the Origins of Mankind by Leslie Aiello (Longman)

Early Man by Anne McCord (Usborne)

Evolution by Colin Patterson (British Museum, Natural History)

Fossils by Mark Lambert (Ward Lock)

Human Origins by Richard Leakey (Hamish Hamilton)

The NatureTrail Book of Rocks & Fossils by M. Bramwell (Usborne)

Man's Place in Evolution (British Museum, Natural History)

Hunting the Past by L.B. Halstead (Hamish Hamilton)

Origin of Species (British Museum, Natural History)

The Prehistoric Age (GBR Educational)

Prehistoric Mammals by Anne McCord (Usborne)

The Problems of Evolution by Mark Ridley (Oxford University Press)

Spotter's Guide to Dinosaurs & other prehistoric animals by D. Norman (Usborne)

Spotter's Guide to Rocks & Minerals by A. Woolley (Usborne)

The Story of Evolution by Ron Taylor (Ward Lock)

The Story of the Earth (Geological Museum, HMSO)

The Theory of Evolution by J. Maynard Smith (Penguin)

Young Scientist Book of Archaeology by B. Cork & S. Reid (Usborne)

Index

First published in 1985 by
Usborne Publishing Ltd
Usborne House
83-85 Saffron Hill, London
EC1N 8RT, England
© 1991, 1985 Usborne
Publishing Ltd.

Printed in Belgium